BELOW THE BELT
COME HARDER

- Devin Hellfire
- Kwoteman
- Carlos Mason
- Brad Crothers
- Tru N Deed
- Christian Thiede
- Jack Veasey

Copyright © 2015 Poem Sugar Press for Community Arts, Ink

Copyright infringement is bad karma. More specifically, all rights reserved. No part of this book may be reproduced, in any form, without specific permission from the publisher, except by a reviewer who wishes to quote brief passages.

Editing by Carla Christopher-Waid w/ T.L. Christopher-Waid and Missi Ritter
Graphic Design, Layout and Cover by Carla Christopher-Waid with T.L. Christopher-Waid
Printed in the United States for PoemSugar Press
York, PA   www.poemsugarpress.com

ISBN-13: 978-0692381144
ISBN-10: 0692381147

BELOW THE BELT
COME HARDER

PoemSugar Press
York, PA

What's Inside...

Devin Hellfire
  Fuck Handcuffs (9)
  Redemption Temptation (10)
  Ardhanarisvara (12)

Kwoteman
  L.O.V.E.J.O.N.E.S. (17)
  When you take time to reminisce (20)
  U So Nasty (21)

Carlos Mason
  I Love to Read (25)
  Passion Fruit (27)
  The Disease (29)

Brad Crothers
  Interchange (33)
  There Are No Rules Here (35)
  Keep (36)
  A Fear Inverted (38)

Tru N Deed
  Before We Kiss (41)
  I'm Not Going to Care (44)
  My Dick (46)

CHRISTIAN THIEDE
- BITTER SOUR TASTE (51)
- RAKED (53)
- THE PRIMAL CALL (54)
- WANT (57)
- MY GIRL (59)

JACK VEASEY
- WHEN I REINCARNATE (63)
- PUBLIC PRIVACY (65)
- MY FIRST BISEXUAL (66)
- JACOB AND THE ANGEL (68)
- PILLOW TALK (70)

Devin

FUCK HANDCUFFS

FUCK HANDCUFFS
I SAID, "DON'T MOVE!"

LISTEN TO ME
LET ME BE THE INSTRUMENT
OF YOUR TORTURE

LET MY WORDS CONFINE YOU
NOT STEEL
NOT LEATHER
BUT ME

I AM THE MASTER
YOU ARE NOTHING
YOU MEAN NOTHING TO ME

I USE YOU ONLY FOR MY PLEASURE
AND YOU LIKE IT
THAT WAY

SO, FUCK HANDCUFFS
I SAID, "DON'T MOVE!"
AND I MEANT IT.

ME AND MY

ROCK

HARD

COCK.

Redemption Temptation

Redemption temptation
Telephone conversation
Come into my church
My temple, my body, my home
Put your long sharp sword
Into me, Joan.

Her touch like fire
Flames licking kicking spitting
Wanting a kiss beginning
Losing my mind
Her hands like magic trying to find
That secret I try to hide

Ripping a hole
into my
fleshy mesh
My chest
My spine
Her fiery fire
Fairy fingers
Wild
Magically
Transforming
My mesh into less
My flesh into fire
My stomach like a hot wire
Coiled around inside

Butterfly wings fluttering
Flying About on a dead end route
Not caring just sharing
Furiously spinning
Lust an evil boy grinning
Winning sinning
Naked truth is trust beginning

Love is stirring up dirt and dust
Mother would clean up
Old sand that is blown inside
My heart and mind
Now and then
Into my eyes

Bringing me higher
Like a freaky infant tornado, in the sky...
touching its tip to Mother Earth
Like this feeling of rebirth

And with every word she speaks
My mind is a whirlwind of pleasure
And I know now, temptations and flirtations
Cannot
Bring about
An Evening
Alone with her
Quicker.

ARDHANARISVARA
(THE HERMAPHRODITE DEITY)

I AM ARDHANARISVARA
EXPERIENCE WITH ME
DHARMA TRANSVESTITISM
CEREBRAL SEX ORGAN MYSTICISM
WALK THROUGH LIFE WITH ME
SPIRITUALLY VIBRATING SEXUAL ENERGIES
AT HUGE INTERSTELLAR FREQUENCIES

I AM THE BEING THAT IS
HALF MAN / HALF WOMAN
I AM THE CREATOR KING & QUEEN OF AMERICA

I AM BREAST & DICK
HARD STEEL & LIPSTICK
I AM THE HERMAPHRODITE
THAT COMES TO YOU IN THE SILVER MOONLIGHT

I AM THE FUTURE THAT IS YESTERDAY
THE SUN BLEEDING ACROSS THE SKY
THE TRANSIENT TRANSSEXUAL ANGELIC WHORE
THE LONG-HAIRED GLAM ROCK IDOL MAN

I AM THE EFFEMINATE
17TH CENTURY FRENCH NOBLE LORD.
PAST & PRESENT ARE SYNCHRONIC
I DRINK TEA WITH MY PINKIE EXTENDED
I ENJOY SEX
WITH HANDSOME STABLE BOY PEASANTS

WITH A DEGREE FROM UNIVERSITY
I BELCH WHEN I GUZZLE BEER
AT THE GAY NIGHTCLUB
I PLAY PARTY GAMES WITH PARTY GIRLS

The World as we know it is coming to an end
I watch it as a stoic statue of freedom
Manhood & macho immortality

I am the girl giggling next to you
I'm laughing at you
your gender stereotypes
Make you small
Insignificant
they flatten the
World.

I am Ardhanarisvara
I am both male and female elements
in all living things
I am the Sky, the Moon, the Earth & the Sun
Round and whole moving faster than
you can see
with naked eyes

My belly gives birth to me
Painful & beautiful birth pains.
I am
Universal
I am
one
Come
pray with me
The Earth
is exploding.

KWOTEMAN

L.O.V.E J.O.N.E.S

I'M ON THIS
LUSTFULLY
OVERWHELMING
VIGOROUS
EMOTIONAL
JOURNEY
OF
NEVER
ENDING
SEX.

IT HAS ME SENDING TEXT AFTER TEXT
SLEEPLESS NIGHTS WITH NO REST
WONDERING WHO'S NEXT.

WILL IT BE SOME BOW-LEGGED MOMMY
WHO LIKES IT FROM BEHIND?
SCREAMS AND CALLS ME DADDY
WHILE CAUSING ME TO BLOW MY LOAD
AS WELL AS HER MIND.

YEEEEAAAHHHHHH, I REMEMBER THAT TIME
I TOLD HER THIS DICK WAS HERS
AND SHE SAID THAT THE COOCHIE WAS MINE
ON THIS LUSTFULLY OVERWHELMING VIGOROUS
EMOTIONAL JOURNEY OF NEVER ENDING SEX.

THEN THERE WAS THIS ONE TIME... AT BAND CAMP...
CHOCOLATE GODDESS
WHOSE HAIR, NAILS AND FACE WERE NEW
AND FROM WHERE SHE CAME, NO ONE KNEW
WHEN I STOOD BESIDE HER
THE DESIRE FOR A TASTE GREW
AND WHEN HER EYES MET MINE
I KNEW IT WAS DIVINE
 INTERVENTION.

I WILL NOT REST UNTIL SHE IS MY QUEEN
AND I'M HER KING AND TOGETHER WE
WILL TRAVEL ON THIS LUSTFULLY OVERWHELMING
VIGOROUS EMOTIONAL
JOURNEY OF NEVER ENDING SEX.

CONQUERING MY MIND, MY COMPOSURE
I SEARCHED BUT COULD NOT FIND
THIS ALL SEEMED TO BE HAPPENING
IN SLOW MOTION INSTEAD OF REAL TIME.

I BLINKED - AND RIGHT BEFORE ME SHE STOOD.

ALL THE THINGS I WOULD DO TO HER IF I COULD
WERE INSTANTLY REPLACED
WITH THOUGHTS OF WORSHIP
BECAUSE A DIFFERENT ROUTE
MY MIND TOOK FOR OUR COURTSHIP.

AS THIS LUSTFULLY OVERWHELMING
VIGOROUS EMOTIONAL JOURNEY OF
NEVER ENDING SEX
INTENSIFIED

HER LEGS I NO LONGER WANTED TO DIVIDE
FOR MY LUSTFUL FEELINGS HAD SUBSIDED
TO MY OVERWHELMING FEELINGS
VIGOROUS I REMAINED,
MY EMOTIONS STAYED THE SAME
BUT THIS JOURNEY OF NEVER ENDING SEX
CHANGED ... TO SERENITY.

I INVITED HER AND SHE CAME,
WHICH PERSUADED ME TO ASK,
" GIRL, WHAT IS YOUR NAME"?

AS WE EMBRACED I LOOKED INTO HER EYES
AND I SAW DESTINY.

When her lips parted
she told me her middle name was Serenity
Right then I knew that my journey
was complete

Because the future
and our children
I could not wait to meet .

It was the first time
I wanted to not only make love,
I wanted to make life.

I've said all that I had to say.
Follow the acronyms.

Anyone can have Lustfully Overwhelming
Vigorous Emotional
Journeys of Never Ending Sex.

but some of us call them
L.O.V.E J.O.N.E.S.

When you take time to reminisce

When you take time to reminisce
the opportunity is there to revisit

Your first and last kiss,
do you remember yours?
'Cause I damn sure remember mine

It was a rainy day in August
when I got home from work
I entered our love nest to air so thick,
to breathe made my chest hurt
I took a deep breath anyway
and collected my thoughts
as well as my things.

With a pain in my heart,
leaving this castle
where I was once crowned King,
the look in her eyes
notified me that my actions
took her by surprise

I paused only to wipe away the tears
 In that moment I realized
we've replayed this scene year after year

With nothing left to be said,
I gently placed my lips
on the crown of her head.

U So Nasty

As I sit, dick hard as shit
with visions of fucking you
Impatiently waiting for you
 to get off work

You walk in, and behind the door I hide
I grab you, kiss you and whisper
can I come inside?

You smile and try to undress
however your French tips and tongue ring
are too busy playing with my chest

On the coffee table we lay, pushing
everything to the floor
SSSSHHHHHIIIITTTTTT!
We're so ready for this
we don't bother to close the door

Off come your shoes,
your stockings, your skirt
One button, two buttons,
then I rip off your shirt

Now I'm like a Rubik's Cube,
because the more you play with me
the harder I get
With all the blood rushing from my head
to my head, I try to hold back a -

A knock and a yell - Dammit!
The neighbors put a stop to our stroking

well, at least now they've answered
"What's all that commotion?"

CARLOS

I Love to Read

You are my A-L-P-H-A-B-E-T alphabet,
And I want to touch you 'til you speak verbs
and sweat,

I wanna devour your text as I skim through
your slim chapters and phrases,
Baby, do you feel my concept?

Let me explore you on the Table
of Contents,
It's nonsense, this constant consonant vow
I have to flip through your pages
front to back, fingers grazing your spine
as I'm reading your vowels,
as I'm reading aloud,

I can't read to myself in my mind,
'cause your plot twists and hot shifts
make it hard
for me to handle your lines

You leave me so shook, shaky,
trembling, achy,
I slowly absorb your
imaginative adjectives
and leave them scattered and fragmented-
on purpose and accident,
reading you as I feed you
my reactions and interjections.

Etched in your sections are beautiful
paragraphs I wanna get in,
fingering your pages
in all directions, these prepositional
phrases so perplexing

I SEARCH THROUGH YOUR TEXT FOR THE CLIMAX
THAT SENDS SHIVERS UP MY BACK

DAMN I LOVE TO READ!
ONE, SOMETIMES TWO BOOKS AT THE SAME TIME
AS I SQUINT AT YO' FINE PRINT
AND BANGIN' ASS LINES
YOU MAKE ME WANNA READ YOU AGAIN AND AGAIN
AND AGAIN UNTIL SEN-TEN-CES
LOSE THEY GRIP AND START FALLIN' OFF THE PAGES
AND SHIT! DON'T….YOU…..
RUN FROM ME.

I WANNA GO THROUGH YOUR LETTERS 'A' THROUGH
'X' TO 'Z'
I MEAN 'A' THROUGH ECSTASY,
I NEED YOUR TRILOGY BECAUSE ONE IS NOT
ENOUGH AND YOU DESERVE TO HAVE MULTIPLE
ENDINGS

I'M BEGGING FOR YOU NOW
AND PLEADING FOR YOU LATER,
MR. ROGER'S LAND OF MAKE BELIEVE-
WON'T YOU BE MY NEIGHBOR?
AS YOU TRAVEL THROUGH MY IMAGINATION
MY CONSCIOUS TONGUE CURLS
AROUND YOUR WET EXCLAMATIONS
YOU CAN BARELY TAKE ALL OF ME
'CAUSE SUBCONSCIOUSLY I'M HUNG

I WANT MY TONGUE TO TOUCH YOUR WORDS
SO MUCH I SWEAR I TASTE YOUR INK,
I THINK OF MADNESS, I SWEAR THIS IS THE BRINK.
THEY SAY THE BEST WAY TO GET RID OF A DESIRE IS
TO GIVE IN TO IT.

SO GIVE IN TO ME, AS I GET INTO YOU,
NOW WHO WANTS TO READ WITH ME?

Passion Fruit

Her kisses tasted like Oranges
Breath like fresh Lime Lemonade in the
summertime

Her nipples were Cherries,
breasts like Melons,
Her butt was an Apple
and it shook
like a full glass of Snapple Iced Tea
Made from the best stuff on Earth, trust me!

Her belly button
possessed the scent of Kiwi
and I swear her Fruit screamed, "Eat Me!"
Calves smooth as Mango
and when she walked her hips
talked and tangoed

How in the world did I ever manage
to hold on to those curves
that flowed like Spanish?
Each strand of her hair
carried the scent of Strawberries
Cada trenza de su pelo,
el perfume de frutillas
tempting me like Roman-god offerings

Her Tangerine tongue would roll
down my Nectarine chest
and across my Blackberry abs
leaving Watermelon sensations in her
reckless sexual path
I would place Plum kisses down her
Raspberry spine

As her moans twirled through my mind
like Grapes on a vine

Her hands rolled
across my shoulders like Honeydew
making me utter, "Damn I want you!"
Her Passion fruit nails dug into my back
leaving trails of Pineapple scratches
as she felt the rhythm of my tropical attack
I turned her over, my kisses leaving
Blueberry patches
down her Plantain back

And when feeling it was right I would give
her Apple a little tap
I would bite into her Cantaloupe neck
Tasting her Pear-flavored sweat
from our cornucopia of sex

As our juices blended we spent hours
getting drunk on each other's Fruit Punch
but what ultimately did me in wasn't
in those Papaya thighs
Amazingly, it was the simple gaze
from her Coconut eyes

The Disease

I have this incurable disease that makes my mind freeze

It makes me wear my heart on my sleeve

And I feel this weakness in my knees

It makes me put up with your bullshit

And you only giving me 50 percent

It makes me try to change for you

And satisfy your every desire even though I know you're a liar

The doctors told me there is no cure for this malignant cancer

That controls my every action
And causes me to find satisfaction in your approving answers

There is no way to get rid of it

While I took my time,
Shared my most intimate gift
To you I was... just some good dick

How did I catch this disease
That makes me stop thinking, stop breathing?
Have dreams of me and you together
In the future with our children
On Christmas Eve dancing
Around Christmas trees with me kissing you

My friends thought that they could save me
from this disease that causes me to accept
when you play me

It clouds my mind and makes me believe
there's no one else for me who
could treat me better

Causes me to write you four page letters
declaring how I feel while
a piece of my soul gets trapped on those
four pages forever

But you give me just enough to keep me

Telling me sweet things like how you really
need me

And what would you do if I were to go and
you were alone

Then ten minutes later you repeat the same
speech to someone else over your cell
phone

We could have been Romeo & Juliet, but
without that tragic death

Since we're not
I will find a cure
for the tortured do no rest

BRAD

INTERCHANGE

The split second
that the match pulled harshly
and gave birth to a fire which lent itself to
become light;

The prayer spoken in slow motion
that tempted the gods to leave the heavens;

The half-closed eyes
you watched the floor with
as it became the sky;

The blur of a repetitive heavy breathing
that simultaneously formed pieces of
broken glass
and ghosts of echoing softness.

You.

Breathing.

Forgotten.

Pulled.

Holy.

The pulsating rhythm of life
beating strong inside your chest;

The foolishness of longing to be anything
beyond the footsteps of this moment;

The melding of flesh and intellect.

I NEVER KNOW IF WHAT I WANT MOST
ARE THE RETURNED BREATHS
THAT PARADE RAGE BETWEEN US
WHILE PUSHING AND PULLING FORWARD TOWARD
SOME GREAT ILLUMINATION;

OR THE MOMENT I ENFOLD MYSELF INTO THE
WARMTH OF YOU
AND CHERISH THE STILLNESS OF QUIET.

There Are No Rules Here

I hear the words
through fear and anticipation
as my mind wanders
into the darkness
behind my closed eyes.
The rough skin of his hands
softly pulled across my chest.

There is a pleading for him to go further;
a longing for him to be nowhere but here.

His warm tongue
leaving trails of lust
before he pulls me into him.
A breath escapes as I let out a soft moan.

There...

KEEP

As vines we overcame.
Entangled and enraptured.
Eyes alike but
aglow with reflections
of foreign landscapes.
We bought into a sky divine
and hid our yearnings from ourselves
in the shadows
to pass.
Escaping spoils untainted by a silence
we still chose to believe in
yet deny.

This is not home,
but a temporary corruption.
A fate denied repetitively;
stagnation;
a silent violence;
stillness.

The noise reduction
we thought was sustenance
erased the whispers
we so desperately needed to hear;
and turned them into muted screams.
It's oddly symmetrical
the way we lie to our inner voices.
The way we dishonor ourselves so easily
in order to avoid that which makes sense.

Slowly we ease comfortably
back into unease.

The death scene daydream.
 The clouds rolling;
darkening;

RECHARGING;
FALLING.
FADING.

THE IMMOLATION OF DREAMS
TURNED TO ASHES AND DUST.
SCATTERED AS MEMORIES
INTO THE INFINITE.

HE AND I
INHALE STARDUST;
EXHALE HISTORIES;
HOLDING HANDS IN THE DARK.

A Fear Inverted

Your eyes
Two identical suns
Setting fire to psychic flesh
Entangled in knowledge
of each other
My eyes
Another hue
Yet linear in their response
Scientific yet religious
An understanding that words and action
are the same with the two of us inside each
other
The tip of your tongue against mine
The depth of my mind in yours.

"It's nothing I can't handle," I say
Truth is I don't want to be able to
I want the fear of pain and embarrassment
To be so great
Yet overcome like
A calm insignificance

All at once

I want my scars
To bear your name

I want to shine
Light into your darkness
And lose the way out

Tru N Deed

BEFORE WE KISS

I FIRST LIKE TO STARE

STARE AT YOUR BARE
LIKE A BEAR CRAVING FOR HONEY
GET LOST
LOOKING AT THE BERMUDA BENEATH YOUR TUMMY
    BE LIKE YUMMY
WHAT'S COOKING
SMELLS DELICIOUS

TAKE LONG MOMENTS TO INHALE YOUR SCENT
NOSE
    NESTLING UP HIGH
FEELING THE HEAT THAT EMANATES FROM
    BETWEEN YOUR THIGHS

LIE WITHIN REACH OF THE TIP
    OF MY TONGUE
AND BREATH
UNTIL WE
ARE EXCHANGING SENSATIONS

ME
WANTING TO INTRODUCE MY SIN
    INTO YOUR NATION
PATIENTLY WAITING

    AS EACH FLICK OF MY TONGUE
    LEAVES A SPOT OF MOISTURE
        IN A DIFFERENT PLACE

COLLECT DATA
ON JUST HOW UNIQUE IS YOUR TASTE
    RECALIBRATE
    AFTER EACH LITTLE SIGH YOU MAKE

                UNTIL THE FIRST MOAN BREAKS
AWAKES

SOMETHING INSIDE THAT YEARNS TO RESPOND IN KIND
FINDS FINGERS
GENTLY MASSAGING THE BASE OF YOUR SPINE
FINDS HANDS
CUPPING YOUR ASS LIKE A GLASS OF RED WINE
FINDS MOUTH
WARM AND WATERING
      LIKE IT'S WAY PAST TIME TO DINE

BE MY DINNER

TONGUE PERSISTENTLY PRODDING
      SLOWLY GETTING ALL UP IN YA

DON'T MEAN TO OFFEND YA
      I'M TRYING TO FIGURE OUT WHAT ARE THE INGREDIENTS IN YOUR DIET
IT'S WONDERFUL TO THE PALLET
          I THINK THAT YOU SHOULD TRY IT

SPLIT YOU WITH MY FINGERS
      ON EACH LAYER I LINGER
LET EACH DROP SLOWLY DRIP
      AND SMEAR IT ALL OVER YOUR LIPS

      BEFORE WE KISS
I'M LOOKING FOR BLISS BELOW YOUR BELT

SIT YOU ON MY FACE
      AWAIT UNTIL YOU MELT IN MY MOUTH
LIKE AUGUST DOWN SOUTH FINDING A PATCH OF GRASS IN THE WOODS
      LAY EXHAUSTED A LITTLE LATER LIKE
          I BE EATING GOOD

WOULD YOU BE MY DINNER?

LET YOUR KISSES BE MY DESERT
        LET MY CURIOSITY MAKE ME A WINNER
          LET ME FIGURE OUT THE CONSTELLATIONS
        BENEATH YOUR SKIRT

BEFORE WE KISS
        BEFORE WE GRIND
          BEFORE I TRY TO MAKE THE MAGIC INSIDE
        YOU BARE

LET'S UNWIND
        JUST POSE THERE
AS I LICK MY LIPS

AND STARE

I'm not going to care...

Hair pulled by the roots
Bitch prolly thinks she was cute
and that cute
is something that would give me pause

When I just want my paws
to have her break out in applause
Cause
ripples...

that can be felt in each nipple
on a mission to cripple,
throwing crumples like throwing humbles

Oh now you wanna fucking mumble?

Had all that shit to say before you
understood my true in deeds don't play
What was that?

Stare at my target like red bulls eyes and
these not so low prices
Oh yeah, it's pretty...

Such a pity
You paid all that money
only for me to get gritty
Latch on to your kitty
and make violins and validations
be smashing pumpkins and calibrations

Have you on my animal planet
Dick harder than granite
Not having sex but more like mating
Debating

Whether this feels like a rhinoplasty
Plastering all over
Or that kingdom of the elephant
Violent in my benevolence

I've conquered like Hannibal
I've castigated like Inquisitions
I've sprayed like I've never been spayed
Ejaculating jokers
That deep dripping flavor like a smoker
Hands work best like a choker
 Call me your personal super soaker

'Cause I'm not gonna care
Give a fuck about your hair
Give two shits about whatever designer clothes you wear
The heels you have
The pocketbook you think looks so good
Whether your inner child is so misunderstood

I'm just trying to get under your hood
And crucify
All over your beautiful eyes
Drip down your hips
As I fit between your lips,
Pry open new realities
And shower you with more than these words
I spit

So make an appointment with your therapist
Don't forget about a mani/pedi
And your hair
Take the dollars I left on your nightstand
And understanding that
I am not
Going to care

My Dick

Tick
Tock
Ticking while I'm licking
We both dripping

Sipping
Sapping
Slapping
Tick
Tock
I'm tapping
Quoth the raven

My dick is a haven
A heaven
Sweet sixteen pounds of pounding
Pungent sounding like bombs bursting in your hair
Over Baghdad
Against the walls of your Troy
Like Cam'ron
Gotcha saying
Boy
Boy
Boy
Oh Boy!

It's thick like oak trees
Long like lassos and nooses
On a seek and destroy mission
For strange fruit and the genome encoding
In your juices

My dick

Dominates dynasties like elephants over the Pyrenees
Like Meroe and Middle Kingdoms
Like Kublai and Akhenaten
Home cooked and hail Marys
Crushes buildings and willpower
Showers golden like gate and bridges
No room for ridges or grassy knolls
Trolls blogs and make dogs growls like
There is an intruder

Built computers
And myths about geometric shapes near Bermuda

Ain't nothing round here short!

My dick
Never aborts
Never gets out of sorts
Never questions
Qualifies
Or quits
Gets
All that it can
Plans and plots

Doesn't have a lock
But is locked and loaded
Not really political
So it doesn't have a button that says I voted
But will accept donations in hard currency
Ain't no soft money
 It's a dark donor
Doesn't mind being a loner
A terrorist
With a ticking time bomb that was the model
For all the obelisks

Bow down before
The catalyst of human history
The driver of procreation and economies
The purveyor of oppression
The genesis of aggression
The cons in our confessions
The reason why it's so hard to learn
The simplest lessons

My dick
Is a national obsession
Exploding and exploring new future
In every Tock
In every Tick
It's constructed pyramids and great walls
Divided people, places and things
Beware of this ticking time bomb
Who knows what next it will bring

CHRISTIAN

Bitter Sour Taste
[Previously published in Fledgling Rag, Issue One]

Your steel wool eyes,
blue-gray and lathered,
look at me
half-masked,
scrape across my face,
and scratch
my eyeballs
with lust.
A couple of tears
escape
and trickle down
my cheek.
You kiss these
damp salty streaks.

You say,
"You know,
he told me
I have perfect lips,
except they turn up
a little
on the corners."
After I came in
your ferocious,
tubular,
aqua mouth,
you declare,
"You looked like
a little baby,
all legs and arms,
squirming and wiggling."
Your small apple tits
bob
before my vision,
your nipples tense,

PINK, AND ERECT—
ERECT LIKE PENCILS
STICKING ERASURE END
OUT.
I LICK
AND SUCK THEM.
YOU EXPRESS,
I CAN
SUCK
MUCH
HARDER
AND EVEN
BITE
THEM.

SO I DO.
YOU GROAN AND
ARCH
BACKWARDS.

UNFORTUNATELY, FOR ME,
YOU ARE A BITTER
SOUR TASTE.

Raked

You raked with your palms,
fingernails, and shiatsu elbows,
raked my scalp receptive,
raked my back grand, groovy, and gorged;
you raked till my skin flecked away
as leaves blowing in the autumn breeze.

You raked with your feet,
calves, and bare parted thighs,
raked my loins musky,
raked my shaft strong, testy, and intense;
you raked till my seed painted
uterine walls with umbrella strokes.

You raked with your tongue,
mouth, and evocative voice,
raked my ears sonorous,
raked my emotions raw, ruby and unrobed;
you raked till I begged you
whimpering as a child to stop.
Then I lie before you
revealed, exposed, and unprotected,
asking nothing,
yet feeling
everything.

The Primal Call

Oh, God, my knees are killing me—
I think they're bleeding.
My elbows too,
but not as bad.

My legs pinned down,
wrapped tight
by her thighs,
   torqued
against the thin, rough
indoor-outdoor carpet.

Her alley cat claws
strafe up and down
my back and buttocks—
I know I'm bleeding there.
I bite her tantalizing neck
and a throaty lioness moan
   escapes.

Our fracas pace increases
turning into pandemonium.

I start to spin,
the speed cheetahs geometrically.
Suddenly, I'm out of control
tumbling over and over,
   over and over,
   over and over.
I do not know which way is up
   nor down.
My warrior battle-cry whoop begins,
soars eagle-like:
Everything blinding light;
   everything pitch black;
Everything blinding light;

EVERYTHING PITCH BLACK.

SOMEWHERE IN THE REMOTE RECESSES,
I HEAR A PRIMITIVE VOICE YELLING.
AS IT TRANSITIONS INTO THE FOREGROUND,
THE REALIZATION FORMS
THAT IT IS
ME,
THE PRIMITIVE YELLING.
ONCE THIS COGNIZANCE CRYSTALLIZES,
I CRASH STONE-LIKE,
MY WIND PUNCHED AWAY.

HOW LONG WAS I OUT
I THINK TO MYSELF?
AND THEN I LAUGH.
OH, I LAUGH,
THE KIND OF LAUGH
THAT ONLY AN EXHAUSTED, HYPNOTIC STATE
CAN RELEASE.
WHEN IT SHAKES UNOBSTRUCTED
THE ADAM AND EVE
IN EVERY PORE ASUNDER.
RETURNS THE PERSON FLAWLESS
TO THE PRE-APPLE-BITTEN
GARDEN-OF-EDEN CONDITION.

I LOOK INTO MY LOVER'S EYES.
OUR VULNERABILITY,
TETHERED BY AN INVISIBLE CORD,
DANGLES.

AND THEN I REMEMBER,
A GURU ONCE TOLD ME
THAT IT IS IN THESE GAPS
WHERE ONE ACTUALIZES,
AND TOUCHES GOD
IN THE MOST DIRECT,

THE MOST PURE,
AND THE MOST COMPLETE WAY.
AND THIS IS WHY WE CRAVE
ORGASMS WITH ALL OUR MIGHT,
VIOLENCE, AND CRAZINESS.

WANT

I WANT TO WIPE
THAT INNOCENCE
OFF
YOUR FACE
FOREVER.
I WANT TO
   RUIN YOU,
MAKE YOU DO THINGS
YOU WILL REGRET FOR
ALL
OF YOUR DAYS.
I WANT TO
   POSSESS YOU.
I WANT TO
   USE YOU
AND SAVAGE YOU.
I WANT TO MAKE YOU
MOAN,
PLEAD FOR MORE,
   MUCH MORE,
BEG ME
TO NEVER
STOP.
I WANT YOU TO KNOW
YOUR DEEPEST
PASSIONS,
NASTIEST SECRETS
   OF DESIRE.
THE DESIRES
YOU ADMIT
TO NO ONE.
THE ONES YOU
BARELY
KNOW ARE
THERE.
THE ONES THAT

ONCE IN A WHILE,
AFTER A SOAKING
RAIN,
YOU CAN SMELL
THE FAINTEST
   OF ODOR.
I WANT TO BRING
THESE
   OUT,
AND HAVE YOU
   CRAVE ME
FOR THEM.
I WANT THAT
DANK,
DARK RECESS.
I WANT TO BURY,
   BURROW
   IN IT,
TASTE YOUR
   LIFEBLOOD,
AND THEN
I WANT YOU
TO DO THE SAME
   TO ME.
HURRY!
COME NOW,
LET'S RUN
   AWAY
   AND FLY
IN EACH OTHER.
THEN MAYBE
WE CAN LOOK
INTO EACH OTHER'S
EYES
AND NOT
LIE.

My Girl

My girl,
my girl is a fiery demon.
My girl is hallelujah hedonism,
a Vesuvius of blazing furor,
a volcano of lusty eyes,
a flame sparking dynamite.
Her lava burns fear.
She is incineration.

My girl,
my girl is a tropical island.
My girl is ripe fruit,
a Hawaii of steaming fertility,
a womb of bloody creation,
a mother birthing life.
Her milk nourishes hunger.
She is civilization.

My girl,
my girl is a blessed-blue wave.
My girl is dolphin's dalliance,
an ocean of soothing support,
a tsunami of sexy sustenance,
a tear drowning despair.
Her love rocks loneliness.
She is celebration.

My girl,
my girl is a musical muse.
My girl is throaty laughter,
a song of crooning harmony,
a chorus of crazy curves,
a siren calling port.
Her voice lullabys limits.
She is liberation.

My girl,
my girl is mine.
She is the world.
She is the one.
She is my girl.

JACK

When I Reincarnate

Forget this New Age princess
Shirley MacLaine stuff.

I want to come back as a biker chick,
Get passed around (at first) from guy to guy
Like a cheap bottle
That tastes better
Than it should. Let me
Get gang banged
On the green felt of
The pool table,
And leave a deep impression
Of my legendary ass. Let me
Rock the clubhouse
So they'll all want
One more taste,
Although they never
Dreamed they would. Let me
Provide the inspiration
For knife fights
Between the Bros,
For tattoos
That immortalize me —
Till that fatal accident
Or liver failure.

I want to be the subject of
A jukebox song, one
Guys will wait in line to play.
Let me be
That mistake
That breaks up
The bland marriages
At last, and
Let me be long gone
When hubby turns around.

Let me leave behind
The mark, the sting, the scent
That sticks
Forever. Let me be like
The road
That left them
Restless.

Public Privacy

When you stare at a stranger —
Unbeknownst to them —
Before too long, they feel it.

They feel stalked, and turn
To check you out,
To meet your gaze.

You look away,
Not wanting to invade —
OK, not wanting to get caught.

Sometimes you glimpse
Their anger and suspicion —
A stranger's admiration

Is not often welcome —
Other times, they just
Seem curious, giving you

Just that much in common.
Either way, the contact
Doesn't last; there is no time

For the unplanned
In modern life. And so,
Unknown potential

Passes by,
And fantasy
Remains intact.

My First Bisexual

The man had a dent in his forehead, due
To childhood
Spinal meningitis. But I fell
For the strange fellow
Anyway. Maybe because
His beard
And one gold earring
Made him look
Piratical.

A potter he was,
And obsessed
About having
A son;
His constant talk about his need
To have a child —
Which he described
As "biological" —
Sounded like he
Had to prove something.

His last name
Was Hart, missing the e
For ease. It was difficult
For him to love.
The dust of his craft
Was all over him,
His hands determined
To shape everything.
After being locked inside
His box of fire,
My eyes glazed over
And I shattered. I suppose
He saw me
As a failed experiment.

My rival
Made a better vessel
For his passion,
With her long black hair
So straight,
And her egg shape.
He told me that his orgasm
Was never good with her —
She'd always have to use her hand
To finish him.
I guess she had
To reach inside herself
For seeding.
Her first name
Came from the Old Testament,
So God
Was on her side —
Or was He? What was that old saying
About tears
And answered prayers?

I saw him
And his son together
Years from then,
From a safe distance —
A little blonde copy
Of him, soft
And ripe
For the shaping.

Jacob and the Angel

They tell you
Jacob wrestled
With an angel.

They don't tell you
It was erotic.

It lasted
All night.
It damaged Jacob's hip
And left him limping —

For no lover
Desires to be forgotten,
Whether human
Or divine

It was significant
The angel did not win;
There was no penetration —
Only orgasm,
Spontaneous
As rain,
Also accompanied
By thunder
(Though it did not wake up
Jacob's wives).

And yes,
The angel blessed him as requested,
But would not tell him
Its name, claiming
Its name was the same
As the place
Where they writhed
All night long;

And he gave Jacob
Also a new name;
Also the name of a place;

As if to say
That where you stand
Is who you are;

And he left Jacob,
Now called Israel,
To live lost
In the ruins
Of their love,
Knowing the man
Would say that it
Was just a battle,
Not admitting
To the kisses
That transformed him,
Claiming rather
That he'd triumphed
Over God, not telling anyone

That God is what you love
In other men, and also
What they love
In you.

Pillow Talk
(or Sympathetic Magic)

My pillow is confused.
It's not used
To the front side of my head,
To slow, sensuous kisses
And caresses.
It didn't know it had a name
That I could murmur into it.
It wonders what
That strange new
Wetness is
Sometimes.

Worse, now it feels
Pangs of its own.
It lies awake
And counts the hours till bedtime,
Lonely for its owner
(Just as he is
For his).

I think about investing it
With magic;
Maybe a lock of your hair
In the pillowcase,
Then, no matter
Where you might be in your travels —
Many miles from me, and even your mind
Elsewhere —
When I wrap my arms around you
You might feel it,
You might think of me
And sense my longing,
Long for me
A little
Too.

DEVIN CHERUBINI was born and raised in the ghettos of Connecticut and lived above the Hell's Angels Club House in Bridgeport. He won awards to study Fine Art and Creative Writing at the Arts at Wesleyan University's C.C.Y, The Educational Center for Art in New Haven, CT and Maryland Institute College of Art. He has been a featured artist and spoken word performer from New York City to Baltimore, MD to Washington D.C. using the stage name Devin Hellfire. His poetry and illustrations have been in various publications and his beat poetry manuscript "Heartbeat" was nominated for a Baltimore Artscape Literary Award in 1998. He produced his own poetry event "From Our Lips" at Café' Metropol in Baltimore for 4 Years. Most recently, he formed the Trans* spectrum conceptual performance art bandTransexual Fetus. He also founded theTrans Baltimore Outreach Society - TBOS, a Baltimore inner city Trans* outreach program offering free counseling to Trans* people.

Thomas J. Tolbert aka Kwoteman, known to most as a military brat, was born in Washington DC. Afforded the luxury of traveling the world, he landed in the middle of Georgia and there began to write. A shy, skinny little kid lacking confidence, he dared not share his stories until one day in 8th grade English when he received an assignment to write a short story and had more words than paper. He put his pen down for almost 15years but was then introduced to a South Georgia group called Poetic Magic. They encouraged him to not only write but to recite. That is when "Kwoteman" was born. Over the next 10 years he performed in Tampa and Orlando Fl., throughout the state of Georgia, the Apache Cafe, Essence Festival in New Orleans, NAACP in Manhattan, and countless schools and venues throughout Pennsylvania.

CARLOS MASON - When I write, I breathe and I'd rather be hated for who I am, than loved pretending to be someone I'm not.

BRAD CROTHERS started a website called Weeping Heretic in 2009, where he shared his poetry. "At the time it was part of a process of erasing myself, and instead became a way to connect. Writing is a way to turn the abstract thoughts in my head into more solidly formed worlds built out of words. Even if the subject matter is bleak and miserable, it offers connection to myself and others. That's why I write."

An economist and systems manager by day, **SHANE TANZYMORE** aka **Tru N Deed** is also an accomplished spoken word artist, venue producer and educator. A member of the spoken word collective and PA Council of the Arts rostered artist group, WordWide, Shane works throughout Maryland and Pennsylvania to support emerging artists of all ages and to bring conscious spoken word to newly appreciative masses.

Christian W. Thiede earned a M.F.A. in Creative Writing from Goddard College in 2009 and is the primary host of Poetry Thursdays, the Almost Uptown Poetry Cartel's weekly open mic. He has performed in venues all around the U.S.A. including Boston, New York City, Baltimore, Philadelphia, Washington, DC, Harrisburg, Montpelier, Minneapolis, Madison, Boulder, Hilo, and Anchorage. His work can be found in the *Pitkin Review, Aquila Review, Cerebral Catalyst, Zygote in My Coffee, Bent Pin Quarterly, Fledgling Rag*, and numerous other publications. He has authored books in both poetry—*Gazing Behind My Eyes*, *Random Poems Now With Homes*, *Confluenza*, and *Little Buffalo Rumblings*—and fiction—*Death and Deception Shake Hands*, *Fools and Love*, and *Aliens, Robots, and Other Haunted Affairs*.

JACK VEASEY is the author of 11 published books of poetry, the most recent being "Shapely: Selected Formal Poems," (The Poet's Press, 2013) and has been featured in multiple anthologies and magazines. His articles on Walt Whitman's life as a gay person were also recently nationally syndicated by The Gay History Project. A frequent collaborator, Jack has worked with photographer Glynis Berger, Theater Center Philadelphia and Theater of the Seventh Sister in Lancaster, as a singer-songwriter with guitarist David Snyder and has released two CDs of original songs. He hosted and co-produced literary radio programs for WITF FM in Harrisburg, and for WXPN FM in Philadelphia; and has been a guest on several radio and television programs including "Culture and Main", "All Things Considered," and "Fresh Air." He is a PUSHCART Prize nominee and has received a Fellowship from The PA Council on the Arts.

WITH GRATITUDE...

The men of *Below the Belt* would like to thank:

Our respective significant others, children, families and friends who have shown us endless support and patience during this project.

The staff of G's Jook Joint, Charm City Kitty Club, The Almost Uptown Poetry Cartel, The Southcentral Pennsylvania LGBT Center and all our friends from the tour.

You! We would all like to thank our beautiful readers for reading, and hopefully enjoying, the collection.

For information on *Below the Belt* tour dates and authors or to learn about forthcoming books in the Below the Belt Series log onto:

HTTP://WWW.FACEBOOK.COM/BELOWTHEBELT
HTTP://WWW.FACEBOOK.COM/POEMSUGAR
HTTP://WWW.POEMSUGARPRESS.COM

Other books available in the Below the Belt series from PoemSugar Press...

Below the Belt (2013)
Below the Belt 2; Go Lower (2014)
Below the Belt 3; Suck-her Punch! (2015)
Below the Belt - Men; Come Harder (2015)

Available at poemsugarpress.com and on Amazon

www.ingramcontent.com/pod-product-compliance
Lightning Source LLC
LaVergne TN
LVHW051156080426
835508LV00021B/2668